I0111767

Here Lies No One

A Poetry Collection

By
B. Brunswick

ISBN: 978-0-6452266-2-1

DEDICATION

To the wounded, the broken and the lost. For those fighting silent battles each day. Never give up because the world needs more good humans like you.

Acknowledgements

I have to start by thanking J.S. Larmore. As much as I appreciate your hard work and understanding of my words, I appreciate your friendship more. My world is far more beautiful for knowing a soul that shines as brightly as yours.

A special shout out to my favourite troublesome pirate, the amazing N.T. Anderson, for a little inspiration, for cheering me on and being amazing. Thanks!

Warning

This book contains some bad language.

Here Lies No One

What do you see at night-time,

I mean, behind the eyes?

Dwelling in your youness, scoffing at the realness

Dark surrounds you heavy, like an iron blanket, pinning
your soul to the ground

But this darkness feels like home

You, mighty soldier of the flesh, child of the cosmos,
unleashing yourself

The planets tremble, and the mountains and trees are
scared to stand in your shadow

Magic rains golden from fingertips

Wonderous sparkles, crackle, igniting a million souls

Nothingness turns to fire and passion, and finally,
echoing laughter

Pouring light, glowing and warming from the smile

The prowlers still linger in the darkness, trying to pull
you in

But you don't fear them any longer

Challenges come and go

You flow down the rapids of life, trying to avoid the rocks that will smash your body to dust

Dragged by the current

Into the unknown

All you can do is prepare

To fight

To push harder

To dust yourself down

To get up again

To keep on going

Determination unwavering

Rolling the punches

A soul that shines as brightly as yours *should* be seen

You will not waver

You surge onwards

Imagine being lost to the world

Never allowing your talents to shine

A destiny unmet

A lifetime unfulfilled

You will thrive

Not die after a life unlived

B. Brunswick

You won't be the one who's headstone reads:

"Here Lies No One"

THE MOMENT

Moments to drift, with time to ponder

Dreaming of the inky yonder

Through child-like gaze, eyes that wander

Heart-a flutters, for a little longer

Green hills roll out to the ocean

Lost in mystery, the silent notion

that blood is warm, no longer frozen

For a moment free from those cold emotions

In this wondrous space the sunlight, warming

Drifting through the hazy morning

Once again, these moments calling

Fluffy clouds in the distance forming

In the breeze the trees are swaying

Amongst tall grasses, butterflies, playing

B. Brunswick

Time seems to linger, forever staying

On soft ground the body laying

As the golden sun sinks, the moon gets higher

Vibrant reds set the sky on fire

This artist's canvas to thrill and inspire

To quell the needs, the hopes, desires

Now ahead the dark horizon

The night of magic, the moon is rising

Stars like pinpricks, twinkling, shining

The planets bright, upwards climbing

Take those moments just to notice

When times seem rocky, lost or hopeless

To change the view, flip the focus

Escaping life when it seems to choke us

The magnificent scene when the world is waking

Quiet staring, when close to breaking

From human woes, this soul's escaping

Just for you, a moment taken

THE MAGIC IN YOU

Memories endless, pain is relentless

Keeps us locked in the dungeon so dank

Taking comfort in pity, in the cold lonely city

Like a pirate we're all walking the plank

We lose all our reason, lose track of the seasons

We lose focus and sometimes we slip

Fading to darkness and twisted by harshness

We are burning and losing our grip

Hanging out in the shadows, heading out to the gallows

Step from the dark to the light

Instead of dwelling in nothing, step out into something

And unleash the magic inside

We may feel like we're losing, but the path that we're choosing

Is winding and it never ends

The storm above rumbles, we're talking in mumbles

B. Brunswick

And tryna hold on to our friends

Sometimes moments just linger, time slips through the fingers

And we're lost and we sway in the wind

Ducking the fury, writing life's story

With the joy and the tears that it brings

The warmth grows inside us, yearning in love lust

The tendrils that spread far and wide

When we feel like we're failing, arms wildly flaying

Unleash the magic inside

We're losing our senses and we're sitting on fences

All to seem as though we are pure

Felling uncertain, doubt drops like a curtain

But we can never admit we're unsure

Fighting and grieving, living and breathing

Can wear us right down to the bone

We'll survive through the sorrow, get better tomorrow

But at that end of the fight is a home

Smoke's thick around us, darkness surrounds us

And times we might just want to hide

But you'll wake to the morning, a new day is dawning

If you unleash the magic inside

Now you will smile and cruise every mile

You're as one with the being within

No longer unravelled, start winning the battle

Take the shots like a champ on the chin

You don't feel you're falling as you find your own calling

You laugh and you work out the way

Some days will beat you, try to defeat you

But now in the past is where it stays

Your armour is stronger, you're fighting for longer

You're confident and swelling with pride

You do life like a boss, a walking colossus

Cos you unleashed the magic inside

B. Brunswick

THE STORM

The patter turns to a hiss of rain

The ghostly clouds in fury fly

A breeze that's cold, that tingles skin

A flash, it cracks the inky sky

A rumble rattles chests and walls

This wild morning comes alive

The trees will bow in fear and grief

And the lightning sparks to life

Sit in wonder, in silence stare

Breathe the rolling mist within

The power crashes right through the Earth

And is carried on the howling wind

Every flash that lights the night

Shows the clouds as their wrath begins

Their fury hot but their soul is cold

The spiteful booming words they sing

The hiss turns to a patter of rain

As the rumbles roll away across the hills

Lining clouds with rings of fire

The wind carries off the harshest chills

The leaves stop their straining cries

The soil is wet from the sudden spill

The morning relaxes once again

After the storm, the world is still

B. Brunswick

Worthy

Wallow, feel hollow

The times that you cried

The scars on your heart

The tears in your eyes

Frightened of being

Afraid of the light

Belong in the shadows

In darkness reside

The traps that were set

Wrap so tight round your soul

The walls hold you in

The pain keeps control

The places you've seen

The dark daunting hole

Where most run in fear

You're taking a stroll

The monsters they came

To rip you apart

To twist you, to send you

Back to the start

To keep you afraid of the light

As one with the dark

And gluing together

The shards of your heart

The tank may run empty

And you keep slowing down

You stagger like a zombie

Through the middle of town

Your legs creak and give way

Leave you crawling around

Breath starts to quicken

Heart starts to pound

B. Brunswick

You're fighting, forever

To stand out in the sun

To hold yourself together

When you ravel undone

Fight through the night

Til the morning will come

If you get through the day

For the moment you've won

You're fighting up hill

The odds against you stacked

You feel like you're shit

But the mirror is black

Reflections in mud

By shadows they're backed

But you are unbroken

Spirit uncracked

There's love that surrounds you

For the most part your blind

There's a warrior's fire

And a gleam in your eyes
You're beauty, you're wisdom
The warmth that's inside
You have that sparkle
Now let it shine

The future is calling
Though the past has been rough
You keep surging onwards
You're getting there tough
You're smiling and strengthened
And more than enough
You'll be as one with your being
You're worthy of love

B. Brunswick

CRICKETS

Empty yourself

Crickets crickets

Chirping like fuck

Darkest place

Never saying a word

Crickets crickets

It's what you give

Not what you take

Wanderer

Warrior

Free spirit

Finding a comfort

But not quite a home

Walker

Rescuer

Crickets crickets

Surrounded by people

Yet somehow alone

Shouting out to

Crickets crickets

Kingdom of sorrow

With an edge of despair

Howling wind

Crickets crickets

Blow a gale

Rips out the hair

Foolish

Forlorn

Cracked spirit

Another blow

And this one hurts

Screaming out

Those fuckin crickets

All they do is

Chirp chirp chirp

B. Brunswick

 # STRANDED

Close your eyes, the silence that deafens

The empty cold feeling again

You're striving along, keep learning lessons

And you won't reach out to your friends

You're out in the nothing, a small lonely island

An ocean too vast to explore

Drifting, so frozen in lingering silence

Cos the waves won't lap at your shore

You're stumbling, and weary and also wind-damaged

You're probing through darkness each day

And the silence is creeping and painful and savage

But you don't even know what to say

Your journey, goes onward, seems never-ending

Your pathway could turn rocks into crumbs

You're a superhero, a warrior, though you're only
pretending

That you can deal with any problem that comes

You seek silence, but seek warmth and love all the same

You'd take comfort in a room full of smiles

When the conversations are starting they could drive you insane

In an instant you'll be running for miles

You drive yourself crazy, pushing your own limits

You stab your own heart with your mind

You think you're lazy, cursed and an idiot

And left kicking your own ass all the time

You cry and wail, when you reach rock bottom

You don't deserve it when it goes well

You may feel empty, and angry, and even forgotten

And the worst fuckin critic of self

Could you hate yourself more, could you drown in your sorrow?

Could you live where the dark spirits hide?

Could you turn out the lights with no hope for tomorrow?

Could you yield to the monsters inside?

Deaf to kind words that come from the others

They never mean them, they want something, they lie

B. Brunswick

When scorned by close friends and cheated by lovers

It's hard not to break down and cry

You are not done, you lost lonely child

There's magic in your being that dwells

And you survived every time, and you fought all the while

To drag yourself out of that hell

You are not stranded or alone, there's people around you

It's not just you versus the world

And if you can reach out, then love can surround you

And just for a moment you're held

The path may be littered with unforeseen resistance

But you, sweet spirit will be fine

Breathe in the light, and burn an existence

And like a star in the cosmos, you shine

LONELY EYES

Sitting there, oh, lonely eyes

Through slumber dreams, the warmth of touch

The truth is told in lonesome cries

Afraid of yourself, so frightened of love

The moonlight's burning brightly now

But through watering eyes, you're missing its grace

The starlight twinkling, wildly now

It's drifting like you, through time and through space

Walking far, oh, trembling heart

You see the vultures though the bird's song is sweet

Your armour dented, soul torn apart

A puzzle so jaded, far from complete

Polish your blade, you warrior

You've come so far, but the battle's not done

B. Brunswick

Take the path, weary wanderer

You're drifting and lost, by cruelty stung

Sitting there, oh angel eyes

Each moment you smile, each beautiful scene

Drifting through sweet lullabies

Growing and learning, to live out the dream

THE BRIGHTNESS OF THE SUN

Look into your soul, you'll find magic

That swirls round your being all day

The good things you do even though you don't feel strong

The words so uplifting you say

You could shine in the night like the cosmos

You could float like a seed on the wind

Not sure how the fuck you can find where to go

When you don't even know where you've been

The morning can come, cold and heavy

And you can curse the fact you awoke

But you'll drag your ass up out of that bed

The only motive you'll need is some hope

Now is the time to step forward

There's a game of life that can be won

And how can you see yourself as invisible

If you burn with the light of the sun

B. Brunswick

Look out to the stars there is magic

In and around you all the time

The cosmos is there, you're a part of it too

But you'd rather live with the demons in mind

Through moments of silence, of presence

You can dream and for once drift away

If you're a prisoner inside of your head

Maybe for a time you can escape

The spirit will swirl bright around you

When by the cold wind, you are stung

But you light up the night like fire inside

Burning with the light of the sun

Look into your eyes there is magic

And a mountain of love in your heart

You can see it, feel it, only then can you believe

When it hurts, you don't fall apart

Pulling yourself up by the boots, to the sunshine

Running around like the breeze

The flowers will smile, birds sing you along

When you smile, when you cry, when you bleed

Tomorrow is beckoning towards you

And it's tempting, and it catches your gaze

And the things you'll dream and then what you do

Will leave you staring, amazed

And the joy will reach out to touch you

You'll be prepared for your time when it comes

You can take it and snatch it, keep it near by

And shine with the light of the sun

Look to the future there's magic

And its motivation is to get you to thrive

To get from the life the things that you crave

And not just barely survive

To dance upon freedom and wonder

To feed off the dreams in your head

To ease off the gravity crushing

And churning full steam ahead

To never give into their envy

To not fight up the tall greasy pole

To fill up the bucket of living

To fill up the hopes of your soul

B. Brunswick

There's a horizon that's begging to meet you

And the million things that will come

How can you fail, or not find your day

When you shine with the light of the sun?

I CAN'T

I can't do this

I can't get it right

I can't be what you want

I can no longer stand and fight

I can't think about it

I can't forget the pain

I can't keep going forward

When I stumble back again

I can't say what I want to

I can't dry the tears

I can't forget the trauma

That's haunted me for years

I can't see where I'm going

I can't tell where I've been

I can't stay standing upright

I can't see the good I bring

I can't get it started

B. Brunswick

I can't see what's ahead

I can't live my life

Not too long until I'm dead

I can't keep falling over

I can't keep warmth inside my heart

I can't see the funny side

I refuse to light the dark

I can't complete the journey

I can't find the way

I can't tell you how I'm feeling

There's nothing else to say

I can't keep it going

I can't take the lumps

I can't get over it

I can't get out of this funk

I can't keep up with progress

I can't hang on the ledge

I can't walk on the razors edge

Without slicing off my head

I can't scream except in silence

I can't take another look

I can't tell my story

It's an empty, dusty book

I can't see the wonder

I can't see the stars

I can't see the horizon

I can't find the path

I can't do this

I can't get it right

I can't stop fighting it

To be happy in this life

I can't give up

I can't forget what I have planned

I can't be weak and afraid

That's the only way I can

B. Brunswick

ZOMBIEING

So silenced by the things that come

The cruel, the fools, the wasted, the dumb

Unravelling seams, coming undone

You sit for a moment, to soak up the sun

While a battle is waging, between the cold and the stung

The weakness, the teardrops dry up, now you're numb

The cracks start appearing, though you hide them so well

A lingering silence that hides what to tell

Untouchable, invincible, yet soft in the shell

High as a kite or going through hell?

You were surging and growing, for a moment you fell

The wind howls so hard while the flood waters swell

Washed up with your reason, washed up on the shore

The soul needs some cleaning, the cold cuts the core

The empty, the wretched, the dead, the impure

Wandering, marching, blindly unsure

Skeletons hammering to knock down your door

Hiding sneaky habits inside every draw

Outrun the shadow, full steam ahead

Stumbling onward, legs as heavy as lead

To keep getting battered, taking blows to the head

You've been broken and fucked up, and you've cried,
and you've bled

One minded, one visioned, surging for flesh

Zombieing forward, becoming undead

B. Brunswick

Human Weather

It's my pain, we belong together

We've been together for a lifetime, the fade in and out
of misery

Joined at the hip, joined at the heart, joined at the soul

Never will be free of it, never it be free of me

It's my darkness, we are as one

Sitting here on the edge of my light, dipping toes in the
frozen ocean

Falling down the slippery slope, sliding on my backside

One with the night, one with the day, one with the sea
of emotion

It's my broken heart, sewed up, jagged, scarred

Beating feebly in my chest, as my blood flows like water
round my veins

Crumbling like a wafer when the shit hits the fan

Twisting round my waking mind, running circles in my
hyperactive brain

They're my twisted thoughts, never owned, just
happening

Taking rides to the water's edge, contemplating once
again jumping in

Running through strange scenarios, ones that never will
happen or be

Taking me down dark alleys, taking headfirst surging
forward, headlong into the wind

It's me, all of it is me, connected together, then to the
cosmos

The light through me runs strong, what comes and goes
is the dark

Stumbling blocks on the journey; rapids down the river
wild

I am strong, I am brave, I am fighting the battle, one
within my mind and my heart

B. Brunswick

PRESSURE

When the whispers come again

They tumble down the mountain

And the face of hope has gone astray

Upon that you were counting

You spin around, in a faceless crowd

Like a coin lost in the fountain

You sit so cold, freaking out

With the troubles that are mounting

A wasted smile, crazy eyes

Your soul is tangled, bleeding

And you smash yourself one more time

The beast inside you're feeding

The gravity, is raining down

Your tired, frame is creaking

And you stare so blank ahead again
There's no point left in weeping

You told the truth, fought with fire
To end up disillusioned
To be tangled up, swept aside
And surrounded by confusion
Cos you're in a place, that shouldn't be
And it is not of your own choosing
You really tried to win this time
Yet once again you're losing

When the night is heavy now
You go through the silence, drifting
The soul and heart will fall apart
When all you need is lifting
You run in mind through the tunnel blind
And your consciousness is shifting
And you hoped so hard for a brighter day
Now you know it's only wishing

B. Brunswick

When the rain is teaming down

And you cower from the thunder

The memories keep a-coming round

And your soul is torn asunder

Waves come to hurt your being

You stagger and you lumber

Crooked backed, but can never break

From the pressure that you're under

Step into the Light

Shadows can hold you

Lock you in darkness

The walls getting closer each day

Thunder it rumbles

Out in the distance

As the storm rips up sea on the bay

Silence it lingers

Long jagged fingers

Illusions that mess with your head

So close to breaking

So close to choking

So close to staying hidden in bed

This may be a stumble

A moment to crumble

But you'll never give up the fight

You'll go forward endless

B. Brunswick

You're tough and relentless

Come and step into the light

At times standing crying

At times standing silent

At times the blood can freeze in your veins

The jagged cold landscape

The visions so hopeless

Flashing time and again through your brain

Locked in a tunnel

What the fuck happened?

Leaves you guessing, recounting the steps

Scars in your being

And your soul endless creaking

And you're dangling over the edge

But you're so far from breaking

You're stronger than you realise

You have grit and fire inside

Not time to give up now

Though you feel so stuck now

Come and step into the light

You feel under rubble

So sad and so troubled

So disillusioned and at the end of your hope

The rain keeps on falling

A flood gathers around you

And you don't even know how to cope

Reached the end of your tether

And try and hold it together

And never show a crack in your shield

Sometimes close to undone

But you stand, staring, numb

Cos you're not even sure how it feels

But you are the spirit

That will go on never quitting

As you head for a future so bright

And you'll answer the calling

The path you are carving

If you come and step into the light

Now the horizon is brighter

The load's a bit lighter

Cos you kept fighting, you could never quit

B. Brunswick

You were sick of being tired

And empty and hopeless

And you ain't gonna put up with their shit

You are stronger and bolder

You are tougher and braver

Than you knew that you could ever be

You can sit in the sunset

Dreaming of the next step

And staring right out to the sea

You can soar like an eagle

You can float on the wind

You can run, you can jump, you can fly

You're shinning so special

You sparkle with magic

Cos you came and stepped into the light

THE PERFECT HUMAN

A soul that needed love

A wanderer alone

Got scars inside my being

Cracks across my bones

Got a million skeletons

Waiting round the bend

I got a million beers inside me

I only need a friend

I got the silent monsters

That whisper up behind

I have a haunted vision

That fucks with my cold mind

I have a broken body

My brain is on the edge

I stumble down the pathway

Of the foolish and inept

I'm a weary, walking, wounded

B. Brunswick

I'm a fuck you from the world

I'm a twat in my mum's basement

That could never get a girl

I'm the broke and I'm the starving

I'm a life that's never lived

I'm the man who ate fuck all

Til I taught myself how to fish

I'm a freak, a fuckin weirdo

I'm the fucked inside the head

I'm the tripping on life completely

I'm the jelly fuckin legged

I've got a back just like a dinosaur

I'm skirting on the fringe

I got a brain just like a fruitcake

And a mouth that has to cringe

I've got a brain the size of a planet

I got Ideas, off the hook

I'm a punch-drunk fuckin fighter

With the million-mile look

I got a thousand discoveries

I got a promise not to break

I got a whole fat load of real

I've got a fat fuckin mistake

I got my soul out in the cosmos

I got to catch my breath

Got an inner clock that's running out

The one sure thing is death

I am merely human

And that's the way I'll stay

But I'll always be striving on

To get better everyday

B. Brunswick

Death by a Thousand Cuts

Drip drip drip

Blood's escaping

Slashing flesh

Close to breaking

The lies unfold

The truth remains

Drip drip drip

Down life's drain

Scream all you like

No one can hear

You wanna ride the night

You wanna disappear

Drip drip drip

Your soul it weeps

The crumbled

Weary

Broken

Weak

Walking hard

Through raging wind

Drip drip drip

The flood comes in

Scars on face

Like a guide to past

Storm clouds looming

Coming fast

Spitting words

Each fresh cut

Drip drip drip

Spilling blood

Stumbling through

Landscapes harsh

Crazy eyes

Maniacal laugh

Concrete prisons

Rock hard luck

Blistered feet

B. Brunswick

Out of fucks

Left behind

Blackened heart

Flaking

Falling

Fading fast

Drip drip drip

Tears leave eyes

Howling out

Haunted cries

Broken heart

A need to heal

Alone

Unloved

All too real

Some days staring

Out to space

Sitting in

The haunted place

Slash slash slash

Til the end of time

Drip drip drip

Your soul it dies

B. Brunswick

TRUE TO YOURSELF

Writhing, so fallen

The message, cold calling

The crickets that chirp round your door

Releasing the feeling

Try hard to keep breathing

And you roll once again on the floor

The streaks in your eyes

The tearless, silent cries

Nobody can know of your pain

You keep wandering on

But in the end, you are wrong

And you're lost in the desert again

Sometimes weakness overflows

But you're letting it go

You must for the sake of your health

Some journeys will end

With lovers and friends

But you have to be true to yourself

The stone statue's cracking

Your strength, you are lacking

And at times you wake up in a hole

While you sit and you ponder

Or the mind starts to wander

But you fight to stay in control

Your shield's bent and damaged

In the battle so savage

You're hanging right onto your grief

Stare out to the ocean

Forget all emotion

And regather your will and belief

The path can be slippery

In a cosmos so tricky

But before you end up on the shelf

Keep moving along

You can't get it wrong

If you'll only stay true to yourself

B. Brunswick

In times that are troubled

The pressure feels double

Find the strength in the core of who you are

You may take a tumble

But the mountain won't crumble

And that's the first step to the stars

At times, out there and drifting

And needing uplifting

And heart fell apart once again

But you still felt the love

When you nearly gave up

Surrounded yourself by real friends

When you want to explode

Stick to your moral code

Don't remember what you lost, but your wealth

Keep ahead of your mission

Believe your intuition

And you'll always stay true to yourself

Treacherous Thoughts

Open

Allow it inside

It flows through the cosmos

No restraints

Not space, nor time

It's beauty, that's silent

It's wonder, it's pure

It can warm up the soul

Or be dashed

Like waves, against rocks on the shore

Thoughts always treacherous

Leaving emotions unchecked

Twisted

Jumbled

Blurred

Reason can fly

And then snowball

B. Brunswick

And fall

There may not be the words

Controlled by the darkness

Consumed by doubt

Swallowed by an illusion

Seeing what will come to pass

In your own tear-filled eyes

Fear and pain and confusion

Looking with a suspicious gaze

At the light, that's shining warm

Smiling

Carving imagined lies

This muddled mist

Of smoke

Of decay

Of mirrors

Of fear

Of untrust

Of pain

Blindly stumbling

Down the hardest fork in the road

Not for the promise of what lies ahead

But the fear that's always behind

Lurking

Creeping

Probing

Clawing

In the treacherous mind

They can jump

They can runaway

They can be stuck in a never-ending circuit

Spinning around

They can grab control

But love

And joy

And beauty

And wonder

Flow through the heart and the soul

B. Brunswick

ZOMBIES

Don't do it man

Don't dwell in the dark

The haunted darkness wants to suck you in

You hate yourself

But you know him

Ripped apart

Howling wind

Dream of glory

Like follies child

Haunting

Taunting

Driving you wild

Lost in rhythm

Lost in despair

Wind chills your bones

And rips out your hair

Crazy child

Scorned

Ripped

And distained

The destiny of blood

Drips cold down the drain

Never enough

Confounded

Contained

Dumb founded

Astounded

Going fuckin insane

Dreams that suck

The fuckin blood out of your soul

The vampires

And zombies

Taking their toll

Like crazy, bleeding you dry

And they swallow you whole

You sew up your eyes

Live in that hole

B. Brunswick

Under pressure

You're longing to fold

Are you still getting better

Or just growing old?

Scars on the Heart

Pick up the pieces

The shards of your soul

Ice over, to keep you alive

Endlessly weeping

When life takes a toll

And you long for the day that you thrive

Sewing up slashes

The ghosts in your head

Put up the walls round your pain

The past comes in flashes

When you lay in your bed

And you've come back to nowhere again

You're wandering endless

Can you get it right?

You're not who you were at the start

The journey relentless

B. Brunswick

That long lonely night

Leaves another scar on the heart

Some people bring darkness

Dressed up as light

Some people use hate as a shield

Sometimes harnessing

Anger and spite

Lies like a weapon they wield

Some people, they mean well

But they're just not that brave

A part of their soul has to hide

They may even seem well

But lost and afraid

And it hurts when you let them inside

Some are broken friends

And they cry out for love

And you try and guide them back on the path

But their trauma becomes them

So it's you that they cut

And it leaves another scar on the heart

Sometimes there's only hope

With a dark cloud of doubt

And it's all you can do to survive

When you struggle to cope

You scream and you shout

Then get back in this fight

Sometimes you're silent

Or you stare out the window

Or you somehow get lost in your head

History's violence

Leaves your face in the pillow

But you fight to surge forward instead

The heart keeps getting stronger

At the times you recover

One day you'll look back and laugh

You bring light where you wander

And give it to others

You need those scars on your heart

B. Brunswick

SILENCE

The dark cloud

Stick that fuckin knife in

Not in the front screaming

But in the back, silent

Twist it

I reel with the pain

I writhe

Turning around to see nothing

Love dashed against rocks

Strength fading

Jagged and spiteful

Cold and wasted

Shivering

Like a whipped puppy

In the dark corners of existence

Under the cloud

The one that follows

Like a shadow

Without reason

Or care for why

Just there

Raining on existence

Soaking the soul

The wounds, jagged and seeping

Tears don't come

Just blood runs from eyes

And puddles

On the wasteland below

The landscape of ash

And decay

Bones picked apart

Crumbling in fury

That has no home

And nowhere to aim

Handing out love on a silver platter

To have it knocked, crashing

To the ground of stone

B. Brunswick

Smashing it apart

Shattering like glass

Thorny chains

The shadow is laughing

Doing right has no meaning

Giving all

For no one

For a dream that was once there

Hasn't faded

But crashed and fuckin burned

And rolls like ashes

Among the rotting corpses of beauty

That twinkle snubbed out

By cruelty and anger

By self fuckin hatred

No value left

It shone golden like the sunrise

Now the night rolls in

Invades the horizon

But the stars have gone

The moon is black

All the wonder and beauty

The night possesses

Invisible now

The dream dissipated

Turned into nightmares

Certainty

Now nothing but doubt

The beckons

And smiles, haunted

Calling me home

Calling me in

In the cave, dwelling

Chewing on bitter fruit

That makes me throw up

Smoke and mirrors

Daggers and shivers

Bloodshot eyes

Gazing onwards and upwards

To that fuckin cloud again

Less than nothing

Not worthy of words

B. Brunswick

Or truth

Or spite

Or venom

Or love

Or anything

Just silence

MASQUERADE

That mask that covers your face, your scars

The lies that you spit to fool the blind

The words ramble onwards, your agenda untold

Covering your soul with a blanket inside

You crash and you burn with regular ease

Ripping out guts as you head on your path

The worst thing to do is to reach out or love you

Leaves scars on the being, and a crack in the heart

The bird of death circles, thick like a cloud

The blood in your veins runs bitterly cold

The smirk on your face as you watch the walls crumble

The mask's on your face, but it can't hide your soul

And flickers of truth, fly by you so quickly

Slamming doors, snubbing it out, erasing your ties

B. Brunswick

And it burns you and hurts you, but you let it control you

The mask on your face, that covers your eyes

And dreams mean nothing, if you don't head towards them

And the endless is nothing, unless you know where you are

Fallen and twisted, and bleeding and lonely

Huddled and broken, battered and scarred

You're running to stay in the welcoming darkness

And all the bad choices, they cut like a knife

The mask doesn't serve you; it holds you there empty

As you break all the things that are good in your life

Beauty could shine if you'd edge out of the darkness

But you'd rather have watched the light flutter by

You're wearing the mask, it's a part of your being

But you are misguided, from yourself never hide

In Hiding

Come out, the sunlight's warm

Come out of your hole

The long endless storm

Come fix your eyes on the day

The world's waiting for you

Your laughter, your smile

The things that you say

Come light up the world with your soul

It's warm and it's bright

Not shady and cold

Come show the humans your face

Show them your mind

Come take your place

Come out of the cave

That holds you inside

B. Brunswick

Come out of your shell

There's no need to hide

GOALS

What are you wanting?

Where are you heading?

Where is the end of your path?

Is it lying your body in a hole in the ground

Or like a warrior reaching the stars?

Is the thunder that rumbles

Through the cold concrete jungle

The thing that will lead you astray?

Is it finding a path, right out of the dark

When you see no other way?

Is it never quitting

No matter what's coming

Is it refusing to yield to your pain?

Is it holding it together

As you piss in the wind

And you're watching it run down the drain?

Is it burning inside you?

B. Brunswick

Is it making you wild?

Is it calling you by name?

Is it calling you on

Or calling you out

when you tremble, so hopeless, afraid?

Is it doubt in the night

Echoes of hate

Or is it whispers of fear?

Is it the beast from the past

Kicking your ass

And whispering into your ear?

Is it a flutter in heart

Or the freedom to choose?

Is it the time to escape?

Is it laughing at you

Mocking you hard

Waiting greedily to watch you break?

Is it too far to go

Too bright to see

Is it the basis of your screams?

Is it giving into your fear

Reach for your worth

Or simply surge towards your dreams?

FALL FOREVER

If the bottom gives out

Could this spirit fall forever?

Wandering around

Aimless, forlorn

If the tears really start

Is there any way to stop them?

If the screaming begins

Swept along with this storm

If the monsters invade

Is there any way to fight them?

Force them away

Yet in the background they dwell

They rush your soul

Every time it's least expected

They linger a while

Leaving a shell

With each misty morning

Does the promise stretch before you?

That promise is folly

As it beckons you in

To save your soul

To give that life some meaning

With a blade in the back

And a cold empty grin

If the bottom gives out

Could the wanderer fall forever?

Bumbling around

With the pain still inside

If the tears really start

Is there any way to stop them?

If the screaming starts

Swept out with the tide

B. Brunswick

How a Flower Blooms

The staring out to emptiness

Stranded all alone

The spite and the hatred

The depression is a home

There's venom in the atmosphere

And it hurts to know it's there

There's a million eyes awaiting your fate

And cruel wind rips through your hair

The mind attacks, the heart burns

The confusion scrambles thought

The loneliness is killing you

To emptiness, distraught

The rubble keeps on tumbling

The misty haze consumes

But you can't let it break you

Cos that's how a flower blooms

Now you drift out in the ocean

It seems you're drawn towards your fate

A head that's in a dungeon

Or a mind that's out in space

You stare out to the distance

The waves crash and then break

The scars are on your heart

And the worry's on your face

You're swaying like the branches

You're creaking in the breeze

You just gotta keep moving

And trying not to freeze

Somehow, keep on going

When a cold tomorrow looms

Cos you're getting stronger daily

And that's how a flower blooms

Could you run a million miles

Leave behind the past?

Could you hang onto your weary soul

Before it shatters like cold glass?

B. Brunswick

Could you run again on empty?

Could you fuck up what's ahead?

Could you stumble down the alleyway

On jelly fuckin legs?

Could you drink away the sorrow

Or crumble at the knees?

Could you stop your heart from breaking

No matter how it bleeds?

Could you face another battle

Before you face your doom?

That is all you've got now

But that's how a flower blooms

Could the darkness break for sunshine?

Could you dare to touch your dreams?

Could the laughter that echoes round the room

Drown out your own screams?

Could you get your shit together

Face up to your fears?

Could you burn bright like you should do

And dry up all the tears?

Could you smile and be joyous

With a twinkle in your eye?

Could your head be in the clouds

When you can reach the sky?

Can you conquer the world

Before you lie in your tomb?

Can you live your best life?

Cos that's how a flower blooms

B. Brunswick

DISCOVERY

Sitting and staring at raindrops on the window

Been jaded and falling, and empty and hollow

The stone heart inside, full of torment and sorrow

You cried out your shame, in the night on your pillow

The skeletons await, and they creep on your journey

Wailing and screaming, and coming, and yearning

They reach for that spirit and this consciousness burning

They reach for that heart just to stab you so firmly

At times in your mind the thunder far rumbles

You're speaking in whispers, as you reason in mumbles

The stairs to the stars, are rocky and crumbled

And try as you might, you can't help but stumble

Mistakes that you make can be lingering, haunting

And the path up ahead looks frightening, daunting

You can't stay locked in your head, like a siren its
warning

And you'll cry out your eyes til the crack in the morning

You try not to break though some people they've hurt
you

You keep telling yourself that they don't deserve you

So you hide with yourself, in this self-imposed curfew

Fighting that darkness that doesn't quite serve you

You listen to echoes from a place in the distance

They call for your soul, it's getting hard to resist them

Are you being the warrior or playing the victim?

You know with each cut, will come so much wisdom

You soul search, your heart hurts, but you keep getting
braver

Take a moment of reflection, each time that you waver

Learning from tears, then turning pain into favour

In the fight with yourself, you can be your own saviour

B. Brunswick

With each lesson we learn, then move onto another

You'll take all the knocks from friends and from lovers

Roll the blow, shake it off, and take your time to recover

Keep striving and surging, climb inside and discover

Devious Reflections

You take your secrets, wear them well

Leaving flesh dangling from your soul

Dust drifts across the landscape ahead

And gathers in your hole

The bell will ring in the distance, afar

For you, forever it tolls

Full steam ahead, headlong into the wind

Haunted gale, stale fear, blowing ever cold

Tracing steps, through landscapes of guilt

Howling into the empty breeze

Jagged memories, twisting your mind

The soul that yearns to freeze

You can stare back at the monster's red eyes

But you can't forget to breathe

You can run your finger over your scars

Drift amongst the jagged naked trees

B. Brunswick

You ride the clock to a future afar

You're old and crooked and just scraping through

And you told yourself you suck so many times

That now you believe it is true

You keep bouncing and swerving and rolling the blows

Never thinking—it's just what you do

But the wolves that came to gorge off your light

Are not a reflection of you

Cruelty raging, breaking your bones

Cold tears will rain from your eyes

Yellow, and fading like the pages unread

The pain, ever dwells in your mind

The horrors cling so hard to your core

And swing on your fear all the time

The things that have happened are not who you are

Now's the time for *your* beauty to shine

CRUMBLING

Silent mist that surrounds, the core of your being

Gormless and staring, can't believe what your seeing

The rumbling thunder rolls into the distance

To go piss its fury on someone else's existence

Each rung on the ladder, slippery and worn

Limping, hunched over, fucked up and deformed

The moments of strength have faded away

The tears in your soul are longing to stay

The gravity's crushing, the pressure keeps mounting

If you're tall as the sky, as big as a mountain

You may be weighed down, and reaching your end

Cos everyone crumbles now and again

The rain whips your face you're stood and you're
swaying

You're a heathenous soul, no point in praying

The wind lashes hard, and screams out it's fury

B. Brunswick

The wall in the path of your own personal story

You can admit it, you don't know what the fuck you're
doing

Are you drinking, and eating and constantly screwing?

Those crazy wide eyes that stare back from the mirror

The surge in your soul from the wild raging river

You're chugging along, though running on empty

You're 40 and fucked so you feel like a century

You may feel like you're broken, amongst broken men

Cos everyone crumbles now and again

The lights flood your mind, and you see where you're
standing

And you position yourself for another hard landing

The trees bow in the breeze, as the storm blows its fury

You're fighting and surging and heading for glory

The last gleam in your eyes is fading so slowly

As you take up your place amongst the lost and the
lonely

Head spins in the crowd, mind flashes endless

The images come and they're fuckin relentless

The tears sometimes fall as you slip to the gloom

But you're not quite ready to fall into doom

You say that you're fine, but your smile is pretend

Cos everyone crumbles now and again

You strive to survive rebuild the foundations

And your pride, running wild all over the nation

The strength yes it wavered, but you found a way through

Keep living each day, just do what you do

The pressure rains down and you're struggling and stooping

But you battle on through, like you know what you're doing

Trying to stand, to keep standing tall

You may be unhinged but your far from a fool

At times life can rip your guts out once more

All you can do is stare out from the shore

And you gather the wisdom from each fight you contend

When everyone crumbles now and again

B. Brunswick

Black Hole

Tumbling through reason

Here we fuckin go again!

The ever-turning seasons

The foolish, the ashamed

Take this torch that's burning brightly

Take this torch and snuff it out

Take this hatred, tall and mighty

Take this venom I spit out

Fuck you for tryna love me!

Fuck you to help me cope!

Fuck you for words of comfort!

Fuck you for all your hope!

I'm a hiding in the shadows

The place that I belong

Standing at the gallows

Singing my moaning, lonesome song

I'm breaking so I'm wailing

So I hate your fucking light

I'd rather sit here fuckin crying!

Hugging my pillow in the night

I hate you, so I'm seething

Cos you tried to save my life

I'm barely fuckin breathing

In this prison I will hide

Fuck you, you soul a-wandering

Tryna fix my heart

Fuck you for believing!

It's tearing me apart

Connecting all the junctions

The cracked circuits in the mind

I can hardly fuckin function

How dare you help me thrive?

You, the one who steps in the nothing

And tries to shine the light

You that's plotting something

By helping me stand and fight

You that gives your all

B. Brunswick

You that helps me stand

You're a stupid fuckin fool!

So, cowardice, I am

You who saw my walls a-crumbling

My tired armour, start to rust

I'm muttering and I'm mumbling

Oh yeah! Fuck you for all your love!

The stars have lost their lustre

But the dark ocean sucks me in

The strength you helped me muster

Is flapping in the wind

How dare you make me need you?

How dare you be my friend?

How dare you speak the truth?

And fuck you once again!

The black hole's fearsome force

The useless light that can't escape

Sucks everything inside

But the darkness still remains

EARTHQUAKES

These stony walls echo silence

Roar like thunder into space

Hunched in the corner, hugging knees

In empty darkness, showing blankly on your face

Arms of warmth that never find you

This darkness deep is your embrace

Tripping, stumbling, falling over

Lagging behind the human race

Heart is cold, soul is bleeding

Tears like ice, from eyes escape

Hanging in the jagged landscape

It's where you're trapped, it's where you're from

The scars mark out where you've been

This floating spirit, does not belong

Inside, you can be trembling like jelly

Outside they will see you standing strong

B. Brunswick

Your spirit sets out to find them

It is evaded, forgotten, and it lingers long

To live by honour, truth and wisdom

And still to fuckin get it wrong

You'll float out to the crystal kingdom

And search forever for a soul that's pure

But you drift away and come untethered

Then get lost, miles from shore

Earthquakes rattle round your being

Then hang on forever inside the core

Blood is black, hardly breathing

And still doing better than before

A human-like warrior, but the battle's lost

Another battle and then the war

The vultures they all circle, crying

Picking the flesh that still remains

Rotten and rancid and covered in maggots

Blood in the soil, empties the veins

Blow out a breath, blowing your mind

Spill out the soul, or scramble the brains

Lurching onwards, unsure, unsettled

Watching the hope, drip down the drain

Feeling the fear, but goes forward regardless

Feeling the moment, absorbing the pain

As hard as a rock, so travelled and weary

As one with the crowd, yet still so alone

The darkness keeps coming til running on empty

Soaked to the core, chilled to the bone

Killing yourself to become all you can do

Melting your heart, not made of stone

Expressions of hope go out in the cosmos

They get tangled, they get lost, and they roam

You're not done, you'll always keep fighting

And maybe one day you'll find what is home

B. Brunswick

COWARD

Here you sit with a shield of distain

Unaffected, unafraid

Ice cold flows the blood in your veins

These unrelenting, concrete days

Tattered pieces that circle drains

Slipping, falling, you dwell in your cave

Closing your eyes to all but hate

Swampy waters, still to wade

Time keeps ticking on your journey to the grave

Jagged branches in the cold wind will sway

Sky is looming, steely and grey

Rejecting wisdom to stay the same

Numb to agony but the trauma stays

A tower of torment, on a pile of pain

Wielding spite like a dagger's blade

Your pathway, with jagged rubble is paved

Your cold lonely bed is so neatly made

You can't get a smile, let alone laid

You don't dream of the light; you lurk in the shade

A million more cruel thoughts that invade

A case on your heart, time bomb in your brain

You wanted some courage but your just not that brave

Caves, ominous that are in your way

It's too hard to heal, so you might as well fade

B. Brunswick

A Vessel for the Soul

You can be battered and bruised

Kicked and abused

The spine could be crooked and hunched

Your legs could feel like lead

Or have an ache in the head

Another day of taking your lumps

You can be sick or so tired

Close to expired

You could be dragging your ass out the door

You can be screaming and crying

Or you could just keep on lying

Alone on the cold concrete floor

You could be on your last breath

Or dangling over the edge

You could be dark, deep inside of that hole

You may feel rejected

But you're out there connected

The body is a vessel for the soul

You can have pain flow forever

While you try and glue it together

You can be coming apart at the seams

You can look to the sky

While the tears leave your eyes

And keep tripping up on your dreams

You can be stumbling, falling

Not hearing your calling

You can keep hitting the block in the road

Life feels like disaster

One never mastered

And you strain under the load

You may feel close to shattered

Like you never mattered

You can be shivering and so freezing cold

The chill in your blood

Leaves you feeling stuck

But the body's a vessel for the soul

B. Brunswick

The rain may fall around you

But you're wading to get through

A life that's so hard and unfair

Legs endlessly aching

While you feel like your breaking

And refuse to get out of the chair

The bones feeling brittle

You're chewing life's gristle

And you're lost in a long lonely dream

Trying to make the most of a life

As one with the night

And trying to learn what it means

You survived every battle

Unflinching, unrattled

Reach out for love you can hold

It's there for the willing

Warm and fulfilling

The body's a vessel for the soul

THE CRACKED MIRROR

Looking in the cracked mirror

Reflection distorted, staring back

Face so ugly, grey and aging

In this fucked-up mirror, cracked

You scold your fragile soul, so scathing

You rumble on just like the storm

And when you're on the verge of breaking

Raging eyes stare back with scorn

Crashing down the wild rapids

Heart smashed to pieces upon the rocks

Solid form that seems to vanish

The hard-battled shell, at once unlocked

The freaking out with hope abandoned

Fucking up what once was clear

Darkness and frustration work in tandem

The warrior, for a moment, a slave to fear

The concrete walls dripping, freezing

B. Brunswick

To trap the soul inside a lie

You ride your feet on the midnight breeze

And you break, you freak, you scream, you cry

A losers mindset gets a grip completely

You're fucked up, useless, standing still

Frail knees tremble weakly

Falling backwards down the hill

But when you're lost, love can find you

Whisper the words you need to hear

That you matter and just remind you

That some days wear smiles, and others wear tears

You wake up to a new horizon

Crystal reflection staring back

Eyes a-sparkle, new day rising

In this mirror that's now uncracked

CHILD

I've been getting lost inside weird daydreams

Running haggard fingers across my scars

So lonesome, jaded, yet restless

Looking helplessly, longingly to the stars

Legs finally creaking, knees buckling

On this journey, endless, I've come so far

So loved and cherished, yet keep on moving

To the irregular rhythm of my heart

Inside somewhere deep I know I miss you

But I don't know who you are

I've been getting lost in moments

In situations and places, I know I don't belong

Yet held here nevertheless, always

As I'm howling out this lonesome song

Stone whispers greet me, welcoming

They come to pull my soul along

B. Brunswick

Screams deafening, yet shrouded in silence
It didn't kill me, neither did it make me strong
Inside somewhere deep I know I miss you
But you were always gone

I've been falling back through glass ceilings
Out to nothing, to darkness, at times I stare
The waves so cold thrash at me, covering me
Leaves me fighting, struggling for air
It's a mystery, what makes me feel this way
No chance of answers, and no clue why I care
Like rubble tumbles, breaks and crushes me
Almost like this life was never fair
Inside somewhere deep I know I miss you
But you were never there

I've been calling out all night to see you
But somehow, every time I've missed
I've been smiling wide to summon you
I've pleaded, fought and wished
I just wanted to take you in my arms

And give that wounded soul a kiss

I wanted to tell you that I'm forever sorry

That I accidentally turned you into this

Inside somewhere deep I know I miss you

But I'm not sure that you exist

I've been reaching my arms out to find you

I call out with nothing but these whispers, soft

Staggering onwards in the howling winds

Toes so bitten, cold with the harsh morning frost

I've been standing in relentless freezing showers

but this damaged soul is never washed

I've been drifting like the tide to nowhere

In this current like driftwood swirled and tossed

Inside somewhere deep I know I love you

But you're the child, lost

B. Brunswick

THE JOURNEY

Forced into existence from nothing, to being

Dumped into this world with the roll of the dice

Love might well just meet you

Or even desert you

Some warmth and some hope would be nice

Hard to believe the things that you're seeing

Those things that slash like a knife

Absorbing lessons

Even those unchosen

Welcome right now, to your life

You wriggle through holes that never fit you

Scraping off skin from your hands and your knees

Weary, forgotten

You're faltering hard

While you fight not to freeze

You're losing your hold on the feeling that hits you

Putting up barriers and trying to breathe

Shallow, so rotten

Falling so fast

Getting so lost in the trees

Teardrops will fall that don't ever suit you

Draining your eyes as you empty your soul

Skirting the edges

Evading the answers

Losing your mind and losing control

They stab you, they rob you, they hit and they shoot you

They put you back down in that hole

Gnawing forever

Slashing with venom

Each shattered heart takes its toll

Each time that you crumble you're frail and distant

Each time you fail, you're barely alive

Lonely and jaded

Haunted and silent

And you'll pour out your pain through your eyes

B. Brunswick

You keep crawling forward, numb and resistant

And the lesson you learn never lies

Crazy and fading

Leaping more hurdles

In the foolish hope, that one day you'll thrive

The mountain before you, seems to always get taller

With another pile of bones in your way

Onwards and upwards

Spiralling downwards

Or one more pathetic display

The storm clouds loom, you keep getting smaller

The same stupid words that you say

Take all they give

Piling upon

Wasted like a ship that's stuck in the bay

These demons march forever and they're coming to get you

You try to run again, but you're standing still

Struggling forward

Stumbling staggering

Limping so lame up this hill

The highlights blend, together they've come to forget
you

They're probing and testing your will

The vultures screaming

Circling, swooping

They're coming to swallow their fill

The moments they linger trying to haunt you

They dream in their scorn for your death

Utter a warning

On a lost lonely morning

And they keep on stealing your breath

The creatures they come to try and taunt you

Or the little of you that is left

They're moaning endless

The zombies relentless

And you're dangling over the edge

For each crack in your existence has left a scar

But left is wisdom and knowledge and strength

Riding the tide

B. Brunswick

Into the shore

When you don't even know where you went

For each track of resistance, burns you a star

The energy that is burning, unspent

Getting it wrong

Getting it right

And you don't know how to repent

You can be cheated or hated, you can see your whole self

You'll be you, when you lie in your bed

Taking a turn

Killing more time

And you can't get it out of your head

You can be laughed at and mocked as you squander your wealth

And those legs are as heavy as lead

Limping along

Dragging your form

Feed off the lies that you're fed

You keep getting better with every pathway you take

You keep etching a map out of scars

Losing your silence

Losing your head

Losing the rhyme of your heart

You wander so blindly into further mistakes

But that's how we become what we are

Taking the lumps

A hole in the head

But cutting a path to the stars

You're evolving and growing with eyes that can see

If you can be honest and never pretend

Loving and trying

Laughing and fighting

And being a wonderful friend

World that's revolving and turning, with eyes that can dream

With a positive message to send

Keep on going

And keep rolling

On this journey that never ends

B. Brunswick

THE END

You shine as brightly as a star in the inky cosmos!

If you enjoyed this book, please leave a review on Amazon or Goodreads today!

Check out: Original and powerful, beautiful and inspiring, take a poetic journey through both outer space and inner, in a thoughtful and uniquely direct way. **Inner Outer: A Poetry Collection.**

For poetry, and wellbeing posts, connect with me on my website **https://bbrunswickpoetry.com**

Other Works by the Author

Out Now!

Inner Outer: A Poetry Collection

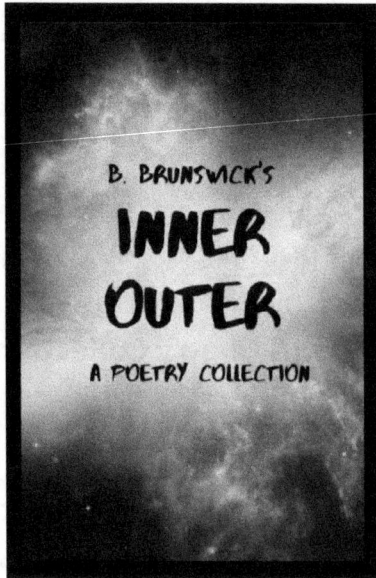

B. Brunswick

Other Works by the Author

Out Now!

The Land Behind the Eyes

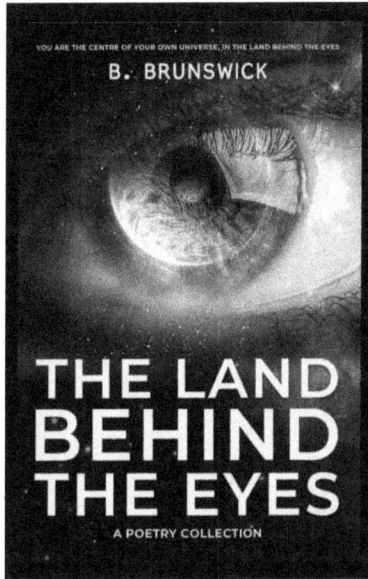

www.ingramcontent.com/pod-product-compliance
Lightning Source LLC
LaVergne TN
LVHW051249080426
835513LV00016B/1828